Published by Write Out Loud,
7 Warehouse Hill,
Marsden HD7 6AB.
www.writeoutloud.net

This edition 2017

ISBN: 978-0-9932044-4-9

Cover photo by Robert Norbury
www.robertnorbury.com

Typeset by Steve at Ignite.
www.ignitebooks.co.uk

Printed and bound in the UK by
Bell & Bain Ltd, Glasgow.

Milestones,
the poetry anthology

Write Out Loud

contents

Milestoners* often wax lyrical about those quirky lumps of rock and rusting iron sitting quietly by the wayside – and the fascinating people who made and who used the highways in earlier times. And what better way to share our enthusiasms than with others who wax lyrical too?! So the 'Milestone' poetry competition was born as part of the 'Finding the Way!' project generously supported by West Midlands Heritage Lottery Fund.

Milestones don't just mark a path into the past, they are also markers on our own timelines, major events.... so participants were invited to write a poem about one or more of them, either literally or figuratively. And hundreds did so! A selection is included in this anthology.

Our thanks are due to the Write Out Loud team who ran the whole completion on behalf of the Milestone Society, to Brian Patten for his insightful judging and most of all to those who submitted entries, with special congratulations to the short-listed winners.

Jan Scrine
Hon Treasurer and Project Manager
The Milestone Society

*Milestoners are members of the Milestone Society.

You can find out more about our projects online at

www.FindingtheWay.org.uk
www.MilestoneSociety.co.uk

We were delighted to be asked by Jan Scrine of the prestigious **Milestone Society** to create and manage this national competition for them, and guessed that using the society's name and preoccupation as the theme - whether the physical entities or their figurative possibilities - would prove inspirational for our many followers. That, and the privilege of having Brian Patten as judge, clearly inspired so many – not far short of 600 entries - to put pen to paper with great skill and imagination.

We are also extremely pleased that our online competition facility has shown its capabilities so well, thanks to our technical director, Paul Emberson, who has worked closely with project manager Steve Pottinger to make it a success. We are now offering this to other organisations who might want us to run a competition for them.

Write Out Loud exists to do all in its power to encourage people to try writing, share their work with others and, in doing so, to find their own voice. As you will see from these pages the standard of poetry and range of ideas, was very high indeed – not least from the under-16s, the winner being a nine-year-old – and it is a shame we did not have room to include more of those wonderful poems in this excellent anthology.

Julian Jordon
Director, Write Out Loud

Notes on the Milestone Competition winners by judge Brian Patten

Adult Category

1st Prize: Track

I was interested that the writer of this poem was instinctively drawn to the Romans. The Latin *mille passus* means - of course - one thousand paces. The endless foot-slog by weary Roman soldiers provided one of our most ancient and abiding units of measurement. (Marching across unfamiliar territory, Roman infantrymen would often drive a stake into the ground to commemorate each thousand paces covered.)

Track explores the downside of this quantification, evoking how the relentless march of so-called civilization obliterated centuries of peaceful footsteps and sacred places with its 'punishing certitude' and trampled on - or marginalised - the natural world. Deftly, the poet segues into more recent invasions, as high streets capitulate to Costa Coffee shops. The form of this poem is perfect - as measured and disciplined as the soldiers' footfalls, and as unstoppable in its drive to a devastating conclusion (progress *'without strategies'*) as any conquering army.

2nd Prize: Cavalry Cemetery, Romania

My choice for second place also has a military theme: a poignantly rural cemetery in Romania where the thirty-three headstones of former cavalrymen become their own milestone of sorts - a symbol of an era where losses could still seem *'romantically fatal'* and individual graves had not yet given way to anonymised *'pits'* of the fallen. I love the restraint of this poem, its delicacy and its moving evocation of the physical reality of each of the impossibly young idealists lying long-cold beneath the flowers.

3rd Prize: Penwith Finger Stone

This poem focusses on a literal milestone in Cornwall, its small-scale granite simplicity set against the vastness of the county's better-known stone landmarks and monoliths (*'Zennor Quoit, Robin's Rocks, Great Zawn, Gunnard's Head...'*) that frame the poem like a shipping forecast. What stands out for me here is the awe of the narrator, his or her fascination and respect for the monument - and the way in which tiny details (was the engraver left-handed?) draw the reader ever closer to the physical reality of the stone and its meaning.

Commended

Dividend, commemorating the opening in 1866 of one of the first of the UK's Co-Op stores, might not seem an obvious milestone. But I loved this left-field approach - and, in fact, the empowerment that the co-operative movement offered to ordinary people (as the poem eloquently explains) was quite remarkable. Despite the century-or-so gap, the breezy detail of this poem whisked me back to my childhood.

In **The Future Perfect Tense**, the milestone is a wedding, but with an arresting modern take as the narrator imagines the newly-weds in the future, interrogating their selfie-stick images of the day - contemplating their own former radiance and struggling to identify unknown faces in the pictures. Close observation and understatement protect the poem from cynicism - even though the final quatrain lingers on other *'many times more married'* couples at the wedding.

Leaving Home's milestone is the departure of a grown-up son from the family home, neatly counterpointed with the remembered loss from captivity of the speaker's childhood pet. What rescues this poem from any hint of sentimentality is the self-awareness of the narrator, who's only too conscious that her son (I'm assuming a female narrator?) is as eager to *'flee'* as her reluctantly jam-jarred lizard.

U-16 Category

1st Prize: Turning Point

In this poem, the 'stone' of the competition's theme is a pebble discovered on the beach; the 'milestone' is the writer's sudden awareness of his or her lifelong fascination with detail, particularly within the natural world. I like the way the poem counterpoints the world of scientific enquiry (*'microscopes and magnifying glasses'*) with lyrical description of nature in its own environment, and also the way that the questions nature stimulates in the writer (*why can't the butterfly be heard?*) lead to fundamental questions about mortality. The stone's colour reminds the poet of the greyness of his or her dead great-grandfather. But, more tellingly still, it is a reminder of the permanence of nature: the poet eyes the *'unblinking'* eye of the stone, and accepts that only the stone will continue to stare *'forever'*. That is the real 'turning point' in this thoughtful and sophisticated poem.

Commended

Milestones caught my attention with its arresting first line: *'I have seen much in my miles'*. The speaker is the milestone itself. Physically, of course, it is unmoving. The *'miles'* it has travelled have been through time, and its journey has been from the early days when it had *'purpose'* to its current lonely fate as *'a mere ornament'* scarred by nature and un-respected by passers-by. The empathy of this poem is very effective (and affecting): the milestone is doomed to eternal solitude, without even the prospect of death.

Grandad Mick tackles the death of a grandparent with forceful clarity, focussing on the physical objects (the watch, the chair, the car) that have outlasted Grandad Mick and are reminders of his absence. Although the poem is framed in the less emotional third person (*'His watch isn't ticking'* ... *'He has gone – nothing can change that'*), at its heart is the personal howl of grief as the second person takes over: *'Your chair is empty now'*. I admire the way this poem's emotion is controlled by its form and the way Mick, its subject, is captured by heartfelt detail.

Malcolm also has death as its subject – the death of the poet's great-grandfather and his or her first experience of the death of someone close (rather than someone less known, and with memories 'invisible' to the writer). In the central section of the poem, the old man's hobbies, habits and enthusiasms are captured in block capitals (*MINT-MUNCHER ... SLIPPER-SHUFFLER ... PEOPLE-CARER*) like entries on a tombstone. But the key focus of the poem is the introspection of the writer him – or her – self, puzzling over a troubling new experience. The preoccupations, colours and imagery of this poem, along with its contemplative beach walk, strongly suggest to me that this poem was written by the author of **Turning Point**. However, it is a separate poem in its own right, and therefore fully worthy of separate commendation in my view.

(editor's note: **Turning Point** and **Malcolm** were written by sisters. Brian was right to see some kind of connection between the two poems)

Main competition
Winners & commended poems

Track

The oldest ones of all crept as wild garlic along the ridge
before the Romans, before the punishing certitude of things,

before hobnails marched reason through the passed-down stories
and trampled neat cobbles over unacknowledged kin,

past the king's wedge-grave and the industrial estate,
both growing ragwort, purposeless, visited by foxes.

The old footfalls are inconsequential now, overlaid, reburied;
still asphalted, here and there, with crazed forgettings.

Along the verges, the shit-sweet smell of old triumph
dissipated into the hayfever of rosebay willow-herb.

Baristas watched the ninth legion passing Costa Coffee;
bindweed fairies saw shopping malls rise, and crumble.

It runs like an autopsy scar on the belly of the country,
a fading jag; flint setts don't regenerate themselves.

Moss and indifference encroach casually over the last beliefs,
without strategies. There's no tramp of pennywort as it marches.

John Baylis Post
1st prize

Cavalry Cemetery, Romania

We came across it not looking for anything
much beyond the battered tower blocks and
empty shops, but a few miles out of the city,
across meadows of poppies and cranesbills
in the corner of an ordinary field under the
slender shade of poplars- a white wooden fence
round thirty or so whiter gravestones, each with a
photo or engraving placed in an oval glass plaque.

Who were they, we wondered, what lost
skirmish had left them in this pretty corner,
the sunlight playing on their sepia faces through
the heart-shaped leaves. Had they died for love
of this place or were they chased here to die
of sabre blows, never to know the name of
this glade that holds their young bones? And

who was it that kept them so clean, repaired
the little plaques, straightened them up so that their
boyish moustaches maintained their equilibrium?
Only the word 'Călăraşi' on each headstone gave
them away. And they looked too smart, too
romantically fatal to be anything else but cavalry.

Thirty three. We counted them. The dead of more
recent wars were thrown in pits, unrecorded. The
Securitati's victims are ash or dismembered limbs
nibbled by fish. They do not signify. So why are these
few dead remembered still, the flowers freshly picked to
strew beneath the plaques that hold their likenesses?

The dead of the Somme too numerous to count beneath
uniform headstones numb to silence the tourists and
school parties with their weight of numbers, their vast calamity.
The thirty three look out, still, from under their busbies,
too young for their epaulettes, no older than the girls
who must bring them flowers, still.

Stephen Devereux
2nd prize

Penwith Finger Stone
Location: SW437374, Treen, beside B3306

Zennor Quoit, Robin's Rocks, Great Zawn
and *Gurnard's Head* ripple off the tongue,
raining their music on this granite land.

I tilt my neck and watch the sky display
its spectral colours as the clouds recede:
two farm dogs scamper up the hill. I walk

towards the finger stone, which hides
between the tarmac and a Cornish hedge:
a snail trail shimmers in the afternoon.

I check the surface of the milestone block.
A hand points to Penzance: it's '6M' up
and over to the arc around Mount's Bay.

This 'stone with benchmark' sends me on
to find a town called 'ƨTIVƨ', without an 'e'
in Ives. Each 'S' is back to front: was this

through lack of learning? It could be
the maker was left-handed for when I
was small and shaping letters into words,

my text ran right to left, which seemed
its natural ebb and flow. I filled the pages
of my stapled book, flicking from the back,

until convention's channels turned the tide.
My current 'S' advances in a coil of surf,
unlike these stone-based characters,

which chime when rain comes pelting
down: *Gurnard's Head, Zennor Quoit,
Robin's Rocks, Great Zawn...*

Caroline Gill
3rd prize

Leaving Home

I kept a lizard in a biscuit tin
when I was small, made it a pool
with jam-jar lid and plucked some leaves
and grass as bed. I stabbed some gashes
in the lid for air and found a worm
and little bugs for food. I came
each hour to see that all was well
till finally it wasn't there. It must have
squeezed out of an over-generous vent
and left my hospitality to be free.

I watch my son cram pillow slip and sheets
into his case, his towel and wash things
firmly crushed into a ball, like courage,
at the top of his bag. My hurried baking
to provide a taste of home, once gone,
discreetly left behind on kitchen sink.
My fussy checks that he'd got all he'd want
annoyed me more than him, catching
vexed sighs and rolling eyes and the need
to climb out of my biscuit tin and flee.

Linda Burnett
commended

The Future Perfect Tense

They will never have been so beautiful
as they are here by the pool taking selfies
on a stick in their wedding clothes together,
white tulle misting over blue water,
morning suit as faint as distant smoke
as the candy stripe golf cart edges into shot.
Years later they will have asked who's the man
with a gloved hand in pink plaid shorts?
Will he have been the secret agent dispatched
to the resort by one of the agencies of despair
with marital bed bombs and mortars of remorse?
Or just another questing American
who's lost a ball and requires the clubhouse bar?
They will never have been so complete
as they are here by the pool taking selfies
on a stick in their wedding clothes together,
white mist, distant smoke, interrupted.
Couples many times more married gaze on,
slung up between palms in rattan hammocks
sipping hi octane cocktails mid-afternoon,
waiting for the cicadas and salted snacks.

Mark Fiddes
commended

Dividend

Moor Lane, Clitheroe – The 1866 Co-op Central Stores

Be born poor two hundred years ago.
Go without all your life. One fine day
appearing on your window-shopping route

are three new shops in a group hug,
their bevelled windows, iron columns
slender as a mill-hand's budget, the décor

drab – to tune with the Queen's devastation
at the death of Albert – five pitiable years on.
Humdrum paint impales the slanting sun

but shoes, cloth, treacle fudge, Ottoman
and Bath chair are affordable all of a sudden.
Dividends provide for, in addition:

Co-op teas "always weighed without the wrapper on",
Lutonia Cocoa (prepared in far-off Luton)
Pelaw Polish buffing its way from Pelaw-on-Tyne.

Onward the Co-op movement steams. You'll find
Butchers at Woone Lane, coal at Sidings,
Grocers with food galore wherever roads join.

Philip Burton
commended

U-16 competition
Winner & commended poems

Turning Point

Another beach walk, combing, looking for something to catch
my eye, why…?
Then stoop, scoop, pluck, hold, see, feel, think. A pebble!
For the first time I find myself
aware that I was always looking closely at things.

Looking closely
Microscopes and magnifying glasses

Like this pasta piece, curled tightly and hard sharp at the ends.
Like long fingernails, like Alice's, my g-gran, Alice.
Like pale yellow light of every morning sun.

Looking closely
Microscopes and magnifying glasses

But why can't I hear the black fly
when it gets stuck in the spider's web, while I
sit silently reading?
Why can't I hear the butterfly, silently
counting the hushed beats of its beautiful wings?

Looking closely
Microscopes and magnifying gasses

The pebble:
made grey, elephant-skin grey, like my dead great-grandad;
the same all around, a mini boulder,
except, a dull chalky white - almost ovoid,
ring around its neck;
one end stubbed, tapered like a big toe.

Its eye caught my eye, unblinking,
And, like me, unblinking, stared,
each at each other, one of us forever.

Still looking closely.

Martha Blue
winner

Grandad Mick

His watch isn't ticking
His shadow isn't reflecting
His heart isn't pumping
His eyes aren't blinking
Time has gone

Why did you have to leave so soon?
There's no king of the family
Your chair is empty now
The family is incomplete

Your car has lost its owner and is weeping in sadness
The grass is growing so long and there's no one to cut it
The flowers have lost their colour just like the house
Time has gone

Your shirts have been turned into cushions
The words on them I know they're true
Because you never wanted to leave

Your watch isn't ticking
Your shadow isn't reflecting
Your heart isn't pumping
Your eyes aren't blinking
He has gone – nothing can change that.

Amber Croft
commended

Milestones

I have seen much in my miles
Of cigarette stubs
Remnants from pipes and cigars
Tobacco laid on the ground in clumps
Like offerings of gratitude for
Notation of my numbers and letters
Travellers must be illiterate to show such credit
Vagabonds, now you mention it

I look back on the day when I was conceived
By the Law of Masonry
Not Freemasonry but
The ones who bruised the frail ground with a spade
For me
Those who rampaged through crowded quarries of hardened
minerals
For me
The ones who shed sweat, blood and tears
With predominant fears
For me
That, was when I had a purpose

But now, I am scarred by mosses and hailstones
Thick as tennis balls
A mere ornament among stacks of reason and rhyme
A mere pawn among a forest of queens
I am there with everything, this and that
That is to say, physically,
In my mind, I am with me, myself and I
Solo right until I die
If milestones die.

Iona Mandal
commended

Malcolm

Rain trickles down my shoulder
and I know I'm getting older.
It's wet and I get it.
Death came to our family. Death of a stranger.

Then a funeral.
A grey stain on my life.
A funeral of strange tears,
tears and tissues passed around
with invisible memories.
Then Malcom died.
Real name Joseph, like his father, like Jesus' father; but
my great-grandad.
GOD–LOVER
        HOME-KEEPER
                ELEPHANT-LOVER
ELEPHANT ORNAMENT–COLLECTOR
            MOTOR–MARVELLER
MINT–MUNCHER   T.V.-TWITCHER
        SOUP–SIPPER
SLIPPER–SHUFFLER
      PUDDING–POLISHER
CRICKET–REVELLER
      ADVENTURE–TRECKER
         FAMILY–ASSEMBLER
ANTIQUE –ENTHUSER   JESUS–FOLLOWER
      PEOPLE–CARER
CHURCH–GOER   VEG–RAISER

Yesterday on the beach
I found something from beneath the waves,
beach-washed like a mini blue whale,
a little shell like an egg, one amongst many, sticking up,

standing out in the crowd,
a mussel shell, dead and empty but beautiful still,
coloured summer-sky blue-grey to chalky-blue
with black and white lines and dots edging it.
Its violet has faded away.
The shape of its curve is ear-like, unique in the shell world;
its stripes equally spaced .
I like this .
If you open it out it looks like open wings of a butterfly.
Puzzled by the puzzle,
puzzling the puzzle each day.
Why oh why oh why won't that puzzle go away?

Aurora Blue
commended

**Main competition
Shortlisted poems**

The Harvest

I want to marry you on harvest morning
When damp presses against windows
And spiders lie flat out in thread houses

In this little church beneath rocks,
beneath sky, beneath God,
the world smells like the earth that it is.

All our futures unravel here,
Where harvest gifts lean up to flowers
And sunlight stacks on a plaited loaf

The years will drop away, unnoticed,
until we lie in state on worn sofas
Old age sleeping on us

As the shadows sag down the walls
Through the hours of a weekday afternoon
Pergolesi will be even more fragile

You'll still be insisting you're a memorialist
I'll still be dreaming up lines about you
And making the tea will be an event

But we will always be the same under older, kinder, skin.

Abigail Meeke

Five

When I realise I no longer know if
Cbeebies are still playing the Spring song
or have changed to Summer
clinging is over, wet wipes almost redundant,
I begin to get crushes on real people
instead of Cbeebies presenters

Nappies gone, buggies folded for the last time
Sippy cup lids linger, teeth-mark grazed
Why am I holding on
To all those coloured plastic spoons?

When uniform time comes
across new thresholds march the fives
soon entering without a backward glance,
so small but full of purpose.
Watch and marvel, as they stop
for conversation with an adult who isn't you.

Hungry caterpillars cast aside.
Bear hunts completed for the last time.

Once I would have cajoled or carried
a night time invader back to their own territory, now I
welcome the intrusion
engulf a tiny body into my own.
Not knowing but fearing
each bed time invasion might be the last.

Alexis Wolfe

Your Point of Reference

When you were thrown out of Eden,
the committee decision stamped out and the doors flung wide,
I was not there to smuggle you back in through the bracken
or, perhaps, over a dry-stone wall.

Finding you, after that day, was a challenge to say the least
and although I like an OS map as much as the next explorer
I know there's only so much that can be conveyed
at a scale of 1:25 000.

Perhaps you hadn't gone far
but had just mistaken the 40 metre incline due south of here
for the 30 metre ascent beyond the river,
or were taking shelter in a building of historic interest nearby.

Unconvinced, the rangers took me to one side and asked,
was I sure that I wouldn't rather locate a lady missing
                                        in grid square 4D
somewhere on a lengthy bridleway, or the elderly gentleman
                                        in 8F
last seen at a current or former place of worship with a spire,
                                        minaret or dome?

By the time I found you at the information centre (seasonal)
you didn't particularly want me to apologise for what had
                                        happened,
but appreciated the risk I'd taken
and hoped I'd had a pleasant trip?

We struck up a conversation for a time,
though the idea of me lifting you back in over the fence
                                was faintly amusing
and when I wrapped my arms around you (to prove I could)

you laughed, and said that you had other plans.

Nowadays, I'm a regular at the information centre
and you drop by sometimes to grab a coffee or a snack.
When you do, I value our talks about the popularity of
                                various nature trails
and how difficult it is to find a quiet moment, in summer,
                                by the lake.

I tell myself you come back more frequently now I'm here,
and hope the triangulation pillar they're constructing nearby
might be an interesting talking point –
at least a place for you to rest on, for a moment, as you pass.

Amy Carbonero

The Impossibility of Return

Nothing had changed. The road down-sloped -
The gulls knife-winged, the chairs sun-striped -
Only the stream was slower now,
Chasing the shadow of the child.

Nothing had changed. Unstable stones
Still candy-skittled underfoot;
Only the mackerel man was old
And mold-and-mildewed, like his boat.

Nothing had changed.
The two Green Swans
Maintain their painful heart-shaped arch;
Only their trumpeting's in vain,
The shuttered inn is cold and dark.

Alisa Lockwood

On Finally Scraping Together Enough Money at the Age of Forty-Eight to Put Down a Deposit on a House

I do not want to leave this house.
I don't want to go and get a mortgage
and buy a different house. I want this house
with its wasabi-infused
chocolate bar in the kitchen,
three squares eaten,
four squares, five…
with its mismatched light-bulbs,
lingering resonance of the smoke alarm
and smell of toast which burned
while the boys were fighting
about who should turn off the grill
just this morning.
With its ticking clocks
each telling a slightly different time,
its sticking light switch, leaking cistern, broken blind.
With its rent paid, cupboards full of food,
 one two three four five six seven eight nine ten eleven
twelve blue-tits in the hawthorn tree
I slashed my arms to pieces cutting back last summer,
with its unsightly rails of drying clothes, its Freeview box,
its Skype,
where everyone who lives with me
still lives with me
and everyone who loves me is still alive.

Cadi Carter Brown

A Man Goes Out

for cigarettes, down Birch Tree Avenue,
left along Queensway, right again. The Co-op
sells Benson & Hedges. First burn, he wants to weep,
sees the 119 bus approach, it slows,
he swings round the pole like a kid,
stairs two at a time, sits at the front.
The bus judders up the hill, diesel stink,
the man takes stock. Behind him,
a mock-Tudor semi, a wife
who won't sleep with him, twin sons
aged six, a privet hedge grown too big.
Ahead, a girl on a stall in Surrey Street Market,
apples in brown paper bags with twisted corners.

Ten years later, two little girls in Milton Keynes
who don't kick footballs, preferring their prams,
shaking their heads when he suggests 'catch'.
He goes out one day, can't buy ciggies –
banned as the girls are asthmatic. He hopes
his boys still kick footballs around the rec,
go down the woods, build dens.

He always wanted to be the dad
who wins the parents' race at sports day,
who hugs his boys; he wanted to be that dad.
He can get on the train and lose his girls,
or stay put and lose his boys.

Another ten years, a bed-sit in Catford, a way
round the edges. Roads wind uphill
and leave him breathless – he's smoking again.
He lingers in parks where boys kick footballs,
little girls wheel their prams. Each drink

dulls the edges. He catches the bus, hops off
at the Co-op, walks up Birch Tree Avenue.

Someone comes out. He knows that man.
Oh God, he knows him, walking
down the street, to buy a packet of fags.
A woman
looks out of the window.
Her face –

Catherine Edmunds

Three Score and Ten: A Life of Biblical Proportions

In my seventieth year I have abandoned nakedness in favour
                         of wyncyette,
Abstain for two days off after every binge,
Exercise my smile muscles for sixty seconds before
                         taking my statin,
Have brunch thus saving one meal a day,
Try to maintain Henry Miller's maxim
                         'Always merry and bright'
After a lifetime of whingeing.
My sexual habits have changed.
Let me say no more.
In Winter I take five minutes in the hour to observe
                         my bird feeders.
In Summer, rain permitting, I wander my garden paths
Musing on passing time.
The arcing sun behind the trees,
The subtle passage of the shade.
I marvel at the fecundity of runner beans,
Question the paucity of peas.
Wonder where all the frogs have gone.
Planning, planning for next year.
No longer so focused on other people's needs.
I work at not feeling guilty.
I accept the past, neither rejecting nor denying it.
I try to keep engaged.
I try to avoid other old people but there are a lot of them about.
I have systems to remember where my car keys are,
To remember my grandkids' birthdays,
To remember take damp clothes out of the washing machine.
So much to remember.
I don't know how I found time to hold down a job,
Drink excessively, stay out to unearthly hours and
Maintain a stable of mistresses.

Incontinence and impotence remind me a clock is ticking.
Vanity is pointless.
No longer the night owl I used to be,
I read late until my eyes droop.
Do I sleep better?
No but my dreams are enjoyable.
Cutting in and out at will
I wait for the day when dream and life are indistinguishable.

Dave Morgan

On top of the mountain, 1956

I love the way you listen to each other
on the phone, keep that hidden speaker on
so you can always hear what I or my brothers
call to ask; how tired you are, how well you slept.

Your face is pink and shiny in the mist, windswept
curls a damp dark tangle on his shoulder, the new
unblemished ring rests lightly on his knee. It crept
up on you, you said; his shy charm, that long tall stride

you still kept pace with right until this year. You cried
out in your sleep again last night, he said. Now I see
how this will go, how one of you will disappear inside
like cloud on top of the mountain. The one left

behind will replay these voices, dust the frame, and
nothing will prepare us for this, the sight of him bereft.

Di Slaney

Baby Tooth

It is a paw reaching forwards,
a mother-of-pearl ornamental claw,
a charm from a mother's bracelet.

It is as sharp and angular
as a snatched hug, slides away to nothing,
the first one that grew, that cut gum.

It is a band of red, then chalk white,
then ivory, the rings of a tree
cut, as if I might just see inside

and find the root, follow the vein,
trace to the core of her
before she is gone.

Emma Hughes

Dear Polly

Sorry I've not been in touch for so long.
A lot has happened since we last met.
I lost my favourite umbrella on a day without rain.
I lost one of my good red shoes on a wild and lonely night
involving roll-mop herring and Quantro.
I lost my husband at B & Q after I spent too long
calculating the currency of shine in the curves of brass cup hooks
and silver bathroom taps. The day after this he left me.
He took the hamster, the car and the bread machine.
I knew he'd not be back so I blended our green Venetian
                              wedding glasses
to a fine, rich powder in the coffee grinder, boiled it up
                              with honey and cream,
lived on it like porridge. I must have been doing something right
because nothing in my body hurt and my throat did not bleed.
I like to think that parts of me are vitreous. On bright days
                              full of sunlight
my fingernails glow like the backs of Tansy beetles.

I had to get some strong men with the right equipment round
to anchor the house down. It kept wandering off.
Usually I could cope with this kind of thing but, I must confess,
I'm not at my best. I was quite distressed when I woke
                              one morning
and realized the house had rambled 26 miles
along the canal towpath to Littleborough. It was a nightmare
trying to get home. The driver wouldn't let us on the bus.
I don't know where it's trying to go. I'm sorry I no longer
                              make it happy.
My mother has suggested that we go to Relate,
                              me and the house,
before things get any worse.

You probably won't have heard but my eyes have gone to the dogs.
I can hardly see anymore but I'm learning to feel my way
                        through the world.
I recognise people by the texture of their shadows.
In a way it makes things less complicated and my sense of smell
                        is so keen now
I can smell someone zesting a lemon in the next town.
                    I can also sense
storms and divorces coming seven weeks before they happen.
My mother suggested I turn this new skill in to a business.

Someone told me that the stars are good and sharp where you live.
Here the lights of suburbia smoke them out.
                        I miss that clean, pure glow
and would love to feel it again on the back of my neck.
                    Could I come and visit?
I'll bring my own glass and a jar of pickled mussels I've been
                        saving for the right occasion.
We can sit on the back step at midnight and eat them
                        with toothpicks
sipping Sloe Gin like we used to before all the husbands
                        and the restless husbands
came on to the scene.

Gaia Holmes

Seven Hours from Home

We've driven seven hours from home
to reach this Welsh shale beach
and the fisherman's cottage above
where my mother's ex-husband
waits at the door, gently scolding
the tiny black cat on the dry-stone wall
beside him, hooking claws into his sweater.

Down by the shushing waves
in hopeful spring sunshine
one standing figure is fishing,
wellies sinking into sand;
my children shriek and rush
the steep hewn rock steps
towards their youngest uncle.

The cat has fled the bustle.
I hug my Dad, standing on the path
he's lined with white crystal shingle.
They pick up moonlight, he tells my husband
so Kingsley and I can find the way from the track
after the pub has shut.
My Dad smells of tobacco,

And through the window I see the pouch.
The cat has moved the tiny shell ship,
the egg-shaped black pebble,
and the china lady; her tail is draped over Dad's pipe
and I wonder if it is warm from being smoked
as he waited patiently
for me to come home
to the house
where I have never lived.   **Emma Hughes**

Forgiveness

And against my will
I took your bad hands in my own
and rubbed them warm
as if I could coax buds
in to your knuckles
believing there is hope of a flower
inside every crooked man.

I stroked milk and Baby Bio
in to your calloused skin
and on the fourth day
there were shy green shoots
nosing their way
through the blood stains,
soft pink petals
blooming beneath your fingernails
and your touch smelled different,
more like the world after rain
and the good soft parts
of spring.

I asked your hands
if they still wanted to kill
and your mouth answered for them.
Pollen came from your lips
and settled on the fields
like gold-dust.

Gaia Holmes

The end of autumn

My father is adrift on the hospital bed,
laid out for visitors in light blue.
Cobwebs of wires and tubes absorb him.
The ventilator sighs evenly.
Gravity shrinks from the room.

My brother and I orbit
the edges of this thinly-haunted body:
warmth in the tight hands,
face flushed like a runner,
its nurse-clipped beard,
- the tricks of dying.

He sleeps under sleep,
his blood wheelspinning
the hours into days.

We hang from the ceiling
for a season. Then autumn
fills and scatters him -

his chest stumbles over the looped air
and breath lets him go joltingly.
He blushes a slow ochre,
the colour of dust,
and a crown of sweat settles on his head.
The digital cry of the heart monitor
flattens to a whine,
switches to silence.

Now the corridors carry us outside.
Morning is pale with winter.
Trees smoulder and splay their old limbs against the sky.
Fallen leaves clump thickly and rot,
their blaze pressed into the ground.

The streets sweep us
through rivers of car light
till we run aground
at our family house.

The rooms burn with the pain
of a phantom limb.
His shoes rest on the rack, lying in state;
his coats hang from hooks, unmanned;
family photographs ache in their frames.

I am suspended in the hallway,
a child again, cradling
the wound that has no cure.

Gavin Bryce

Welsh Alec

He was one of those people who grew better looking with age,
time was a friend, snow white hair, pink shirt,
distinguished, debonair,
a poor man's David Niven

'He doesn't take life seriously' my sister worried
'look at the state of the house, its falling down'
but my father had other gifts to share

gregarious, flirtatious and sociable, at ease with his
                                light-hearted life,
but his piece de résistance was dancing
a smooth foxtrot, a nimble quick-step, an elegant waltz
Welsh Alec danced well

and the women came in droves:
Betty, Sally, Alice, lovely Alice, Vera, Miriam, Joan,
                                nightmare Joan
My father was a widow's dream, his little black book overflowed

We danced through my childhood together,
cocooned in a safe world of MGM make believe
                                and long-limbed dancers
on a black and white screen:
Rita Heyworth, Cyd Charisse, Ann Miller and my father,
a poor man's Fred Astaire

'Tell me about Wales, Dad' though I knew the stories off by heart:
running over the mountain to school
midnight poaching with his Da
the poverty, the strike that led to leaving the valley
                                to move up north

losing his accent so he wouldn't get teased
and teaching me to say
'llanfairpwllgwyngyllgogerychwyrndrobwllllantysiliogogogoch'

Later came wartime tales of North Africa, Italy and Salerno
no bad memories shared,
camaraderie, good times and the humour of his pals,
discovering melons in Alexandria
going AWOL for mum's birthday,
witnessing the Glenn Miller concert,
a poor man's Ronald Coleman
All this and the early death of my mother, his own Ginger Rogers –

Welsh Alec made a choice to enjoy life, to keep it light
'bugger the house' he'd say 'lets go dancing'

When he died my sister and I worked through his little black book,
the women came to his funeral in droves:
sad-eyed widows, and married ladies lingering in the shadow of
gravestones

my father taught me to dance the foxtrot, and so much more.

Hilary Walker

Remember Me

Do I know you dear?
The question she asks
me every morning
with her lemon smile
and tepid eyes.

'I'm Denise; your daughter',
I say to the empty space
between us.

I wish she'd had a sudden death and
not this sleeping sickness
that makes a drought
of memory.

I show her photographs:
My first birthday,
First day at school,
Graduation,
The wedding.

I want to plant a seed
within her frozen womb,
Let her recall that first flicker,
How she touched her belly
with a secret smile.

Remember the pain of labour
as she struggled to give birth,
Held me against her swollen breast
with joy.

Let her start again
from *my* first breath,
Return to find the child in me,
The awkward adolescent,
The middle aged woman
Who longs to be hugged.
Start the journey of *our* past
again.

'Are you sure?
I thought I had a son.'

Jacqueline Pemberton

Swimming lessons

As we meander back to the car
I tell you how good I think you are now.
Become an otter to my land loving eye,
sleek as you slip through the surface,
a sheen like oil, legs gently pulsing,
flash of the tail to glide you along.

You look thoughtful and proud. We chatter on.
Your brain is expanding in a big bang
of enquiry, avid for new matter,
Drawing complexity in. You wonder
if there are other planets on which,
the lesson just done, a man much like me
with a girl talking just so, are making
their way down a street indistinguishable
from this, conversing, holding hands,
bag swinging, wet towel and cossie within,
goggles in their case, shower of rain passed by.

We talk about possibility, maybe an infinite
number of us doing the same, more or less.
Daughters who are learning and growing.
Fathers who know as much as I know and that's it.
A multitude of men who are weak swimmers,
fear open water, vast limitless space.
Who guide these girls a while then cede,
adrift in love without measure, treading water.
Watch as the strong young arms
Scythe the oncoming tide, part the water ahead.
As you trust my words and then let them go,
Float away, set sights on the future's shore.

Giles Constable

Last night we were undressed by the wind

It took our shoes first;
we watched them rise like odd dense birds
into the indigo sky.

It undid buttons, habits, words;
twirled away the shadows on your face,
the lines engraved on mine.

It freed the magpie in your ribcage,
unzipped each one of my muttering scars, opened our heads to
the blazing dark.

And then there was only bright skin.
And then we were
just air.

Last night we were undressed
by the wind. This morning
we woke in our clothes.

Janet Lees

The three ages of woman*

Although your days only orbit mine now,
I thought I saw a glimpse of us in the postcard you sent.
Its corners were scuffed by heat and sand,
by rubbing against other people's bills and love letters.
Yet   for a moment   the painting told our
story.
I felt again, the damp fluttering of your eyelids against my
throat,
the tangle of milky fingers in my hair.
I wonder whether there are flowers where you are,
strange and exotic perfume in the air as you sleep.

*Painting by Gustav Klimt 1905

Jennie E. Owen

When I retired I thought

perhaps I'll learn to draw like Durer,
craft colour like Matisse,
disentangle shape Picasso's way
and shock the taste police,

perhaps I'll be an actor
as versatile as Streep,
hone tragic parts like Bernhardt
and watch my audience weep,

perhaps I'll be a singer
angst-driven like Piaf,
or purr vocal wit like Eartha Kitt
and make my groupies laugh,

perhaps I'll be a writer
with the status of the bard,
as political as Miller,
as prolific as Stoppard,

as familial as Heaney,
as funny as McGough
with Oscars for my screenplays
and Baftas by the trough ...

so I bought the oils and painted,
joined a group who improvise,
wrote poems and rhyming ditties
that have never won a prize,

sang pop at the College of Music,
riffed jazz along with the prof -
life's choc-a-bloc with learning
but Baftas are a long way off ...

Kathy Osgerby

By the Old Airport

Hong Kong, 1987

The rooftop terrace where we stood face up to the bellies
of descending planes, 150 feet above, blocking our sky;
their thunder filled our ears and throats
as they swooped down to the final approach,
five miles to Kai Tak runway. Expats ourselves, of a
different sort, we asked: was he Scottish and homesick,
the man who named this spot Grampian Road?

Yesterday, I googled you and also our old home.
There are cafes on the road, did you know? Savills
sells new developments. 'The Grandeur.' Of course.
Our flushing system never worked, the drains continually clogged,
the paving around our building so uneven, I tripped often.
My scarred knees still know it. You are an interior designer
in a city I've never visited. One reason we haven't met since then.

The Baptist church across our old street is now shiny new,
doors of polished brass and glass; it has sprouted offices
around the modest cream cross that rises above. Unchanged.
Oh those hours you spent, my dear flat-mate, at the window
gazing at the brides on the church steps, aah-ing at their
lavish white dresses, their signature poses:
with groom, without groom, with family, alone.

Alone on the steps but not lonely, always the same photographer
arranging their arms and bouquets; serious, unsmiling, clicking.
At your window you sighed misty-eyed, judged: this dress too frilly,
that train too long, the white not bright enough, the lace bell
sleeves you would love to have. You sucked in your cheeks to pose
for the photographer's busy back. We knew that you would marry
in red not white, around a fire and not on a Sunday. Yet.

The street behind us filled with a string of hairdressers, I got
a sharp new bob, styled by the young apprentice who took
too long but gave me a haircut everyone remarked on.
Google shows me a hotel occupying that row. Contemporary.
It's not like the one we went to for the smorgasbord brunch, the spicy
bloodymarys, the dim dining room with secret mould in the corners,
our overloaded plates, our grins reckless towards our sedate futures.

Kavita A. Jindal

Raven's Last Journey

Perched alone on the milestone,
the spy considered offers from fylgjur,
haunting the woods like fox wraiths.

Night worn as a cloak, tired bones aching
under old breeze ruffled feathers,
his conspiracy was betrayed
as silhouettes in tempered moonlight.

He watched ghost clouds, drifting like lost leaves,
disturbing stars suspended on the edge of eternity.
At midnight, revealed by bright flecks of white,
his gift from the gods in polished beads of jet,
he contemplated his own last flight home.

But dawn found him sightless and stiff;
a raven's lights extinguished. This rag by the stone;
a journey of fifteen years from his birth
in the boughs of Yggdrasil,
where he'd first told Odin
the secrets of men.

Jonathan Humble

That Moment

Just at that moment when the train pulls out –
That fatal jolt – when, craning, I see you
Waving at me, I'm overcome by doubt;
I find that all I ever want to do
Is shout out *Stop the train!* It seems the cost
Of leaving is to realise what I've lost.

This longing always grasps me at the end.
I used to wish that it would let me be,
But after many years, I comprehend -
I did not know my deepest treachery.
Once I was blind, but sweetheart, now I know
That moment is the reason that I go.

Lindsay Reid

Watchful

A neighbor, elderly lone bachelor
is taken in turns by other neighbors
to the doctor, a hospital bed, back home,
the grocer's, again the doctor,
the hospital, home from there

We offer covered dishes
of stews saltless fatless cheerless
nourishing him for the next trip
to the doctor, the hospital perhaps home
but never again the grocer's

Today I have for him dessert --
a chocolate pudding bereft of sugar
and gluten but – grand treat! – a single
almond topping very lonely up there
and even then maybe threatening

My David makes a turn slowly too slowly
into oncoming traffic, not seeing
the car whose lane we are encroaching
and again I begin numbering
the other times he has done this

Our scenes are tilting. He was so strong
He taught me to drive, he moved people
as you do chess pieces. He wrought feats
of romance shifting continents to reach me.
We have traveled so far to this point

There are more signs creeping
 into our life together, no clear signal
 I am receiving yet my eyes perceive absences,
a halting, a response borne with effort
and so I make ready for our new adventure

A duty of love, a crowning of our history,
our drama heading for another chapter
without recourse yet somehow completion
I am present, seasoned, girded, watchful

Lucilla Bellucci

Station of the Cross II

Remember that time
when Sarah Pickles, Queen of the Playground Regime,
called you "blackie",
and your boss, King of Office Banter,
said "it's ok, darkie",
or that time when Fast-Fingered Francis
aimed for your skirt
jeers dancing behind you
'til you reached Salem Avenue.
Or when Nasty Nick, that rolling stone,
dumped you
without the decency to phone.
Remember the fibres
from that overcoat of shame,
how they clung to you
in your poor-hood again,
living on cherry jam and bread,
leftovers from lovely Mrs Brown downstairs,
her kindness catching you unawares.
Remember how your tears rocked the stairwell
when grandma died,
and the land meant for you
robbed by relatives you never knew,
or when your uncle said "good riddance",
"goodbye",
told you not to return,
because you were different, you see,
educated, too highbrow
to be part of them now.
Remember each break,
and humiliation's song,
those choruses of life to all belong,

arteries of rejection and restrain,
how they crossed,
bringing something new
to carry you through.

Mariama Ifode

Passport

So Staff Nurse Sue hands me a duplicate canary
yellow form, *The last thing before you go*, echoes
in my mind, as I cross the crowded foyer, pass
the bee-sting flower stall, the humming escalator
hear the creak of signs for x-ray, E.C.G. burrow
deeper and deeper into the ship's hold, until I find
The Hall of Lifts. Full stop. Don't forget to breathe.
Pressed behind a woman on a stretcher, a porter
and two doctors deep in consultation, we ascend
spilling out on Level Five, where I sway down
the longest deck towards Wards 44 and 45, opposite
the airless cabin, where Claire first unrolled
the book of charts and diagrams. All along the way
I wonder How good to have this latest advance –
a passport-sized photo stamped on an identity
card, pinned on your gown. No need for constant
questions: Your name? Your date of birth?
No need for the empty wristband.
I reach the door marked Post the Form and Knock.
As the clock strikes two, a young girl leads me in, takes
my coat to hang up in reception, asks me to wait beside
the wooden bench. That's fine by me. Gives me time
to comb my hair, dishevelled,

                            slightly seasick

by the patient morning

                          the tramline marking up.
In the silver mirror I paint my lips a deep plum
add a layer of mascara.

                    I want to look my best
A tall woman with a heavy camera strapped
around her neck, appears. She gives her name.
Jessica. I give her mine. We smile ready for the shot.

She tells me to step over to the full length screen.
Stand on X.
As I move forward, before the shutter falls,
                she calls out *Take off your top.*
                  Don't forget to breathe

Pamela Gormally

Auntie Miranda

It was a journey through the living room
to the scullery - bare brick, the top-half glassed. Cold

creaked through the frames. Standing at the pot sink
she would gaze into the garden. On Mondays

she was planted on the concrete floor, possed washing
in the dolly tub, her knuckles barnacled

round the pole. Stalk thin, in slippers with bulbous lumps,
she crabbed down steps to the washing line, bent

to pluck slugs from cabbages, lettuces, picked sticks
of rhubarb she charmed into soft suet puddings.

One day, Great Aunt Miranda's bed came downstairs.
There she lay, like driftwood, for everyone to see. Looked

through glasses so thick, her eyes were far away. In a photograph
on the sideboard, she has hair like a mermaid's.

Lynne Taylor

Filament

Come summer, with all its itch and abundance,
we'll drift these mardling lanes late into evening, casting
left-handed folk songs and inventing collective nouns:
an orogeny of matters; a hinterland of wants;

an atlas of us.

The boys will brash ahead, carrying sticks
and self-fulfilling prophesies. Becoming their own
waymarkers and measures of distance. Late-up, wild-fired
vigour machines, contradicting the darkening sky. Outrunning

all the old futures.

I will venture a mapless compliment: *of course
I love you, you are my nemesis*. Or some such. A smile
will regather your face and the day-drunk sun
will make filament of those strays of hair,

escaped from your ties

to recline and kiss the curve of your neck
like free-verse. Like lazy dissenters. And, come
summer, with all its itch and abundance, we'll remember
this about this place in which we have chanced root:

there are no mountains,

and what we call hills here are only undulations.
There are hares afield, harriers aloft. Latent desire-lines
await the shape of our tread and our singing. To lead
us and to follow us to wherever it is we are going.

Paul Howarth

Packing it in

I'm packing for our 25th anniversary
school reunion and it's proving painful.
I'm carefully placing the old school tie next
to an apology to the boy
who won't ever go to a reunion,
and wondering how I might get it to him
and why he won't be on the year-by-year photos
on the display boards when we stand
next to them with pints and glasses and sighs.

I'm not actually wondering this.
I'm wondering about my life
after his life and the *roll, don't fold* advice
from the packing website.
I feel folded and unable
to roll with things.

Next to my toiletry bag I'm slipping
in the small photos of individual classmates
and the note to my English teacher
which begins with *Sorry*.

The big guy from further south
who joined our class when we were thirteen –
what will I say if he turns up?
Should I check for bruises?
Will we crowd round and point
out the scars?

I don't know if he'll be there because I searched
for him online and found no trace.
I've been thinking about buying
him a replacement briefcase
and filling it with better memories.

I'm walking too slowly to the car
and the case is feeling very heavy.
I'm opening it and wondering about taking
something out. I'm weighing up the tie.
It's been knotted for twenty five years.

Rob Walton

Marching with my granddaughter

& I am the Oompa
& I march & I march
& strap the teddy in the pushchair when I take her to the shops
& am not scared of anything, except when she says *Boo!*
& can find missing Lego, pencils, drumsticks & spoons

& I am the Oompa
& I march & I march
& know the names of the seventeen cuddly toys she adores
& before she sleeps I must carry the noise of sunlight away
& make the sound of everything in the world, even dinosaurs

& I am the Oompa
& I march & I march
& have to keep fit by swimming & going to the gym twice weekly
& it doesn't matter who says *Snap* first, she collects the cards
& I pretend not to know that she's hiding behind the settee,
as always

& I am the Oompa
& I march & I march
& can buy toys I always wanted – a Gruffalo puppet, magic
sketcher
& she gives me her hand & we march down the steep staircase
& when she calls me a *Silly Oompa* I want to march
& march forever

Rodney Wood

Of Love & Sex, & the Problem of Gendering

They've got it wrong, the Germans, naming
the beach as masculine - *der Strand* – when,
just strolling along Formby foreshore, shows
it's clearly female, wide-eyed and going deeper
than surfaces. They're daft, too, neutering

James Joyce's "scrotum-tightening" sea into
a sexless *das Meer*. For one, it's all woman,
with her cockteaser attractiveness under rain
as getting testily-petulant she turns down sand;
and, two, when the tide's full out, and its etched

horizon is miles away, (whether it's scorching
sun or louring cloud that threatens) she makes it
worth your trekking there to taste her allure.
Once back on shore again, they're partly right
with dunes – *die Dünen* - their shifting plurality

like recumbent sculptures of lossocking women
their limbs trickle-lifting, rising and falling
as if disturbed mid-dream, then resettling,
while keeping close to chest those ruttings and
rootings of natterjack toads and marram grass.

And can't complain about what they've done to
sand - *die Sand* - as it slips womanly-vulnerable
through fingers, like love - *die Liebe*. But then,
being English - masculine, feminine, whatever –
love is love: just that - the sex already understood ...

Roger Elkin

Old as Brass

Old lady hunched
in the pew, curled
on herself like
a French horn,

arthritic hip all that keeps
trombone husband from
sliding proud about town
with her, arm in arm.

Best friend beside is
more of a cornet, more
tightly wound; holding
all her widowed self in,

just waiting
for the solo
to be over.

Sally Davis

Stones

I carry stones in my pockets to keep
myself weighed down, my feet
from tiptoeing.

I leave small stones beside the path
to mark my way, to show
I've been there.

I put a stone on my father's grave
to let him know I am still here
and I remember.

I put a stone, another and another on
my mother's grave, on the double
depth of her and him.

I drop stones from a bridge to hear
the water swallow them,
hear it say *forgive them*.

Susan Utting

Furthest East

This is about as far as England goes- tiny
tongue of sand and boulders stuck out
at the North Sea. Here there's none of
the drama, the hype of a destination
that Land's End and John O'Groats do so well.
No one knows where it is quite, the
Ness more of a line on a map than a place.
The council had to put up a plaque.

A few beaten up trawlers nudge each
other like dozing cows as the harbour's
greasy swell cuts under them. They nod through
dreams of great storms, heroic catches.
Old men come to look, recite the sacred names:
Gypsy Queen, Pegasus, Saint Mark.
Only the sleek yachts tug on their leads, long
for the sea, demand attention, devour the light.

The fish went north years ago along with the
offshore rigs and the money. In the flaking
canning plant pallets of tinned peas rust silently
in the darkness as the swing-bridge's arms rise
like rusted lobster claws.

The kids are less benumbed, get on with the
business of smoking crack, shagging in the dunes,
signing on. They gaze over the sea wall to
where they'd been told there were dykes and
clogs and windmills, where now a continent
recedes, turns its back on them.

Only on sunny days, when the abandoned
factories and slipways display their
vivid, separate failures do families stroll
down to the dazed beach with their tea,
mallets and ragged windbreaks. Beyond
them the harbour's arms still make their gesture
of welcome, embrace the empty horizon.

Stephen Devereux

Scaffolding

Today he smiled for the first time.
Today he rolled over, back-to-front.
Today he crawled.
Picks daisies out of the grass.
Toddles, unsteady. Babbles, falls over.
Discovers and destroys dandelion clocks.
Points at pigeons with both index fingers
Chases them into the air.

In the petting zoo behind the museum,
Points at the soft, quivering rabbits.
Tugs and pushes the wire fence;
Weak, ineffectual.
Inside, points at birds behind the glass.
Slate blue passenger pigeons,
Copper blush, smog-grey, faded.
Slaps the glass with open palms, softly.

He doesn't care for toy birds in the gift shop.
The taxidermist's art compels.
Something of the imitation, intimation,
Scaffolding of life remains.
Doesn't know yet the eyes behind the glass
Are also glass.
The wings neatly folded for a hundred years.

Sharada Keats

Tick Tock

You're counting up the numbers, one two three,
and sounding out the words with a joyful glee.

I catch you in the morning testing out the fours,
walking down the hall I see you auditing the doors.

Eight's become a favourite, a word to shout out loud, but
seven, more elusive, still hides among the crowd.

You reach up with your digits and I keep them in my hand,
I draw along the lines and trace a journey yet unplanned.

And we will count together as the hands tick tock, your
story here unfolding, a whole world to unlock.

Tatterhood

Thirteen

"You're a woman now!" my father teases,
proud smile on his face.

I try to suppress the shudder
those words engender in me.
Words I've heard before.

My eyes meet those of my uncle...
his hold no warmth,
his interest in me waned
with the onset of breasts and periods.

I'm too old for him now.

"You're a woman now!" he said
to me when I turned eight.
That birthday 'treat' that was no treat.
Not for me at least.

I used to think monsters hid
beneath beds and in wardrobes.
but real monsters dwell
in men, not shadows.

My monster's eyes drift away.
I see a smile at the corner
of that hated mouth.
My youngest cousin
has caught his interest.

She is seven, full of innocence
and cute smiles, as I once was.

I have kept this secret too long.
I must save her.

After all, I am a woman now.

Tracy Davidson

What Is Write Out Loud?

Write Out Loud is a national (indeed, international) hub for participation in poetry, encouraging everyone who writes poetry – from still-too-nervous-to-do-open-mic to Nobel Prize winner – to share their words with others.

The **Write Out Loud** website has been around since 2005. It's unique in what it brings together, and what it offers to our members. Here you'll find our unparallelled news section (covering news from publishers, poets, events, gig reviews and book reviews), our gig guide (where you can find out what's happening near you) and, of course, our blogs (where you can post your work, and read and comment on work posted by others).

All of this is designed to encourage interaction in a comfortable and inclusive atmosphere, which helps explain why over 45,000 people visit the website each month, and why they keep coming back.

Join them at **www.writeoutloud.net**